Cosmic Cocktails

A GUIDE TO THE MIXOLOGY OF ASTROLOGY

LYDIA LEVINE

summersdale

COSMIC COCKTAILS

Text by Abi McMahon

An Hachette UK Company
www.hachette.co.uk

Summersdale Publishers Ltd
Part of Octopus Publishing Group Limited
Carmelite House
50 Victoria Embankment
LONDON
EC4Y 0DZ
UK

www.summersdale.com

Printed and bound in China

ISBN: 978-1-80007-552-8

Substantial discounts on bulk quantities of Summersdale books are available to corporations, professional associations and other organizations. For details, contact and general enquiries: telephone: +44 (0) 1243 771107 or email: enquiries@summersdale.com.

Disclaimer: The publisher urges care and caution in the pursuit of any of the activities represented in this book. This book is intended for use by adults only. Please drink responsibly.

Contents

*⭐ Introduction *⭐

Welcome to *Cosmic Cocktails*, the book that charts the zodiac and offers customized cocktail recipes for each star sign. This little guide uses modern astrology to help guide you as to your place in the universe. It invites you to look inwards, at your traits and behaviour, and learn more about yourself.

Once you feel better connected to yourself and the universe, it's time to start making cosmic cocktails that have been carefully chosen for you. You'll find a short menu of cocktails under each astrological sign: some will be familiar friends, some may be future favourites, but all will give your taste buds an out-of-this-world experience and help bring out the best in you.

Try them out and transform your evening into a spectacular soirée.

✦ How to Use This Book ✦

This divine book is divided into the 12 signs of the zodiac. Each chapter contains an overview of the key traits, including strengths and weaknesses, of the astrological sun sign, rising sign and moon sign. It also features a short section describing what each sun sign is drawn to and turned off by in friendship and relationships. You can create your very own cocktail menu by searching through the book for your sun sign, rising sign and moon sign's cocktail recommendations. What's more, each section contains an additional cocktail "potion", designed to help bring out the best in you and your personal connections.

✦ Astrology: The Basics ✦

Western astrology is based on the notion that everybody's personality is informed by the date, time and place of their birth. These factors determine your sun, moon and rising placements.

THE 12 SIGNS OF THE ZODIAC

The 12 signs of the zodiac are the 12 constellations that the sun, moon and planets travel past (or appear to travel past) on a path known as the ecliptic. The connection between the real path of these celestial bodies and the path mapped on astrological charts is approximate, smoothed out for ease of measurement. The word "zodiac" means "circle of animals", which is reflected in the symbols that represent each astrological sign. These signs are: Aries, Taurus, Gemini, Cancer, Leo, Virgo, Libra, Scorpio, Sagittarius, Capricorn, Aquarius and Pisces.

Each sign has a sun, moon and rising variation. Although there is a strong thread connecting these three variations - for example a Pisces sun and a Pisces rising may both be dreamers - the celestial object in each sign will impact the strength of these characteristics. You can easily calculate your birth chart by entering information into an online birth chart calculator.

ELEMENTAL TYPES

Each zodiac sign is divided into one of four elemental types. These are: earth, air, water and fire. Each element carries its own traits that, when combined with the influence of the stars, form the basis of your character.

Earth: Taurus, Virgo, Capricorn. These signs tend to be grounded, prize stability and exercise caution.

Air: Gemini, Libra, Aquarius. These signs are outgoing and idealistic. They intellectualize their emotions and are happy to go with the flow.

Water: Cancer, Scorpio, Pisces. Water signs use their intuition and are extremely empathetic and sensitive.

Fire: Aries, Leo, Sagittarius. These signs are quick to action and enjoy staying active. They value spontaneity.

SUN, RISING AND MOON SIGNS: WHAT THEY ARE

Sun: If you are new to astrology, your sun sign is probably the one with which you are most familiar. It's defined by the position of the sun in the sky when you were born, usually determined by your date of birth. Your sun sign usually represents who you are at your core; the traits you find there are the ones that drive you – the habits that you keep returning to. However, your sun sign doesn't represent all you are – how could it, when you are such a multifaceted being? If you have ever felt that your sun sign doesn't fully portray you in your entirety, look to your moon and rising signs for more nuance.

Moon: Your moon sign is also determined by your date of birth. It's most deeply connected to your emotional nature. You might notice that the traits you find in your moon sign reflect the way your emotions flow and the way you prefer to express them. Your moon sign contains the key to the ways you need to be emotionally nourished in order to grow. You'll also notice that your instinctual reactions to situations reflect your moon sign nature.

Rising: Your rising sign reflects the location of the constellation on the eastern horizon at the time of your birth. It's important to note that the location and date of your birth impacts this. Your rising sign is often the first face that you present to the world. It's more curated than your other sign behaviours, and you're better able to choose who sees it when. But just because it's easier to control these behaviours doesn't mean they, or the sign, are any less authentic. Your rising sign reflects the elements of yourself that you admire, that you would like to hold on to and be known for. Some people feel most closely connected to their rising sign self and consider it their "true" self.

✦ Cocktail-Making: The Basics ✦

An entire universe of out-of-this-world cocktails are at your fingertips and all you need is a handful of specialist equipment.

EQUIPMENT

Cocktail shaker: Cocktail shakers come in many varieties and are an efficient and stylish way to combine ingredients quickly.

Jug: Sharing cocktails contain large volumes of ingredients and need to be prepared in jugs.

Strainer: Cocktail ingredients are usually shaken together with ice, to chill. The cocktail is then poured into a glass through a small, fine strainer to separate the liquid from the ice, fruit pulp and other unwanted elements. Some particularly delicate cocktails require a fine-mesh sieve.

Muddler: A heavy mixing spoon with a weighted end to crush solid ingredients. Used to crush sugar and fruits or bruise fragrant herbs such as mint to release the flavour.

Bar spoon: A long-handled spoon designed to reach the bottom of a cocktail shaker or highball.

Jigger: A double-ended shot measurer: one side measures a "single" shot and the other a "double" shot.

Glasses: Some cocktails are short and powerful, others are long and refreshing. Serve in the right glass for the right effect.

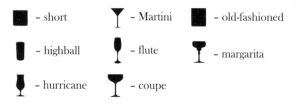

■ – short   🍸 – Martini   ■ – old-fashioned

▮ – highball   🍷 – flute   🍷 – margarita

🍷 – hurricane   🍸 – coupe

Techniques

Like astrology, cocktail-making comes with a language of its own. The following list describes certain techniques that are referred to throughout this book. If you find a term you don't understand in the recipes, check back here for the "how to".

Layer: Recipes will tell you to layer the ingredients when they need to be added in that exact order, without pre-mixing or stirring after. For example, it's the layering of the ingredients that gives a tequila sunrise its pretty ombré appearance. For best results, pour the liquid into the glass over the back of a bar spoon.

Muddle: Stir heavily, crushing soft ingredients, such as fruit and herbs, and grinding hard ones, such as sugar and ice.

Shake: The most common term in cocktail-making! Shake the ingredients together by combining them in a cocktail shaker, usually with ice, closing the shaker and giving several good, hard shakes. Hold the shaker in the air for added flair.

Stir: Stirring is called for when a cocktail can't be shaken (or you like your cocktails stirred, not shaken). For example, if a cocktail includes fizzy beverages, such as champagne, shaking will eliminate the delightful fizz, but stirring will combine the ingredients and preserve the bubbles.

Strain: The second most common technique. Place the strainer on the glass and pour the ingredients from the cocktail shaker, through the strainer, into the glass.

⋆ Top Tips for Cocktail-Making ⋆

- ✦ Put cracked ice in your glass, unless the recipe says otherwise. Crushing to a pulp or leaving the ice cubes whole isn't encouraged; by cracking the ice cubes, the optimum surface area is gained. This will make the cocktail's temperature and consistency just right and will ensure the drink is neither too diluted nor tepid before it is served.

- ✦ Simple syrup can be easily made at home. Add equal quantities of water and white sugar to a saucepan and simmer until the sugar is dissolved and the mixture is slightly thickened.

- ✦ Nearly every item on the equipment list can be replaced with common household items, so you can get started on cocktail-making right away. Chopsticks can become a bar spoon, shot glasses become jiggers, wooden spoons or pestles become muddlers and a tea strainer becomes a cocktail strainer.

- ✦ Glasses can be chilled by simply placing them in the fridge, if you have space. Or, fill with ice and leave to stand for around half an hour before use.

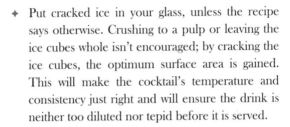

Aries

(21 MARCH – 19 APRIL)

RULING PLANET: MARS
ELEMENT: FIRE

✦ Sun Sign: Overview ✦

Aries suns are bold and brave. You know what you want and you prefer to forge your own path to get there. You're happy to bring others along with you as you're a natural leader. You're also a bit of a charmer and your vibrant energy can fill a room. You're ambitious and your plans are big – when you make plans at all. Aries suns are spontaneous – sometimes impetuous – and full of enthusiasm for your next big adventure. If a cocktail could embody an Aries sun, it would be effervescent, bursting with striking flavours that jostle for dominance.

PERSONALITY

Shyness isn't something Aries suns suffer much from. You are assertive and, when full of vim and enthusiasm for your latest project, feel practically invulnerable. This feeling of invulnerability can be a great asset, but sometimes your light shines so brightly that you struggle to see your own flaws. Your honesty is admirable, preferring direct and frank communication, and you're always looking for your next big project to put into action. It's between projects that your spirit starts to get restless and you start to search for the next bit of fun.

LOVE AND RELATIONSHIPS

Sun-sign Aries have big hearts that you wear on your sleeve for all to see. You're always ready to take a big romantic leap and fall in love. Such passion and enthusiasm is hard to resist and new loves – and new friendships – are easier to come by for you than for most others.

Even though you're a force of nature, you don't mind being checked – in fact you like to be challenged. It doesn't faze you, perhaps because you've always got an answer for any argument. Your charm means that it's rare for people to mind too much when you lock horns with them.

With all that get up and go you need someone to match your fire. You haven't got a lot of time to pick over the faults, whether they are your own or your partner's. A self-assured Leo makes a good match for you. When it comes to friendship, you crave a partner in crime, someone who will match you step for step. Earth signs are too change-averse for you, but a Gemini could keep up with your energy.

✦ Rising Sign: Overview ✦

As an Aries rising you're refreshingly candid – it's rare that anyone is left wondering what you're thinking. You tend to act first and think second. Sometimes this works for you and sometimes you have to use your considerable charm to get out of a tight spot. Either way, you usually end up getting what you want. For all that you're independent and impulsive, you play surprisingly well with others. You have a deep respect for other people and you're a great teammate.

✦ Moon Sign: Overview ✦

Aries moons are full of feelings and led by emotion. This is good when you're on the up – small moments can lead to bursts of joy – but it can mean you find yourself consumed by negative feelings. You're quick to act on your emotions, and sometimes you don't look before you leap. Still, this means you're often a pioneer, the first to try something new. You don't like to mince your words and will say things as you see them.

Nobile

Bold flavours and a striking colour – just an Aries sun's style – this cocktail is sun-kissed with summer flavour!

EQUIPMENT

- ✦ **Cocktail shaker, filled with ice**
- ✦ **Strainer**
- ✦ **Highball glass, filled with ice**

INGREDIENTS

- ✦ **20 ml (⅔ fl oz) vodka**
- ✦ **20 ml (⅔ fl oz) red amaro**
- ✦ **Splash of limoncello**
- ✦ **40 ml (1⅓ fl oz) orange juice**
- ✦ **40 ml (1⅓ fl oz) raspberry juice**
- ✦ **Bitter lemon to finish**
- ✦ **Sprig of mint to garnish**

METHOD

Combine all ingredients except bitter lemon and mint in the cocktail shaker.

Shake until combined and strain into highball.

Top with bitter lemon and garnish with mint.

Bunny Hug

Aries suns are all about action, and you don't get much more action-packed than this gin, whisky and sambuca cocktail. This will get you going, if it doesn't stop you in your tracks.

EQUIPMENT
+ **Cocktail shaker, filled with ice**
+ **Strainer**
+ **Martini glass**

INGREDIENTS
+ **60 ml (2 fl oz) gin**
+ **60 ml (2 fl oz) whisky**
+ **60 ml (2 fl oz) sambuca**

METHOD

Add the gin, whisky and sambuca to the cocktail shaker.

Shake until combined and strain into chilled Martini glass.

Boom!

Jalapeño Mockarita

Only an Aries sun would be crazy enough to try this one – serve this mocktail to attract fellow adventurers.

EQUIPMENT

- ✦ Saucepan
- ✦ Sieve
- ✦ Chilled Margarita glass

INGREDIENTS

- ✦ 250 g (9 oz) sugar
- ✦ 250 ml (8½ fl oz) water
- ✦ 6 jalapeño peppers, sliced
- ✦ Crushed ice
- ✦ 6 mint leaves
- ✦ Lemon and lime soda to top
- ✦ 50 ml (1⅔ fl oz) lime juice

METHOD

Prepare the simple syrup by heating the sugar in the water until the sugar dissolves. Taking the saucepan off the heat, add jalapeños and lime juice and let steep for 10 minutes, then strain into a jar and place in the fridge.

Muddle handful of crushed ice and mint leaves in chilled glass.

Fill the glass halfway with the syrup, then top with lemon and lime soda.

Fuzzy Navel

A quick and easy cocktail recipe for the quick-to-act Aries rising sign. The fuzzy navel is short on prep time but long on flavour.

EQUIPMENT

+ **Cocktail shaker, filled with ice**
+ **Strainer**
+ **Highball glass, filled with ice**

INGREDIENTS

+ **60 ml (2 fl oz) peach schnapps**
+ **140 ml (4⅔ fl oz) orange juice**

METHOD

Shake to combine the schnapps and juice.
Strain into the glass.

Squashed Frog

Aries moons are straight shooters, so here is one of the tastiest shooters around. (A shooter is a long-layered shot served in a tall or "double" shot glass.)

EQUIPMENT
+ **Long shot glass**

INGREDIENTS
+ **15 ml (½ fl oz) grenadine**
+ **15 ml (½ fl oz) melon liqueur**
+ **15 ml (½ fl oz) advocaat**

METHOD

Layer the ingredients carefully in the glass. The bottom layer is grenadine, the middle melon liqueur and the top the advocaat.

Taurus

(20 APRIL – 20 MAY)

RULING PLANET: VENUS
ELEMENT: EARTH

✦ Sun Sign: Overview ✦

As a sun-sign Taurus, you are patient and you enjoy the finer things in life. This means that you won't mind waiting a little longer – or working a little harder – for the best-tasting cocktail. It takes a while for you to make your mind up about something new but once you do, you're all in – and you stand firm by your favourites. However, don't be afraid to try new things – today's new experience could become tomorrow's daily routine.

PERSONALITY

You find strength in your routine. You love the sense of personal security – something you value highly – that comes with being sure of your path and knowing what comes next. That said, change can scare you, especially when it comes with little warning. You may dig your heels – or hooves – in when it comes to changing your mind, but people just need to be patient. New friends and loved ones may be surprised the first time you go all out to make things happen, but they'll soon learn that there's no obstacle that can't be overcome with a little Taurus gumption and magic.

LOVE AND RELATIONSHIPS

Warm-hearted, trustworthy and loyal – it's a pleasure to be loved by a sun-sign Taurus. You may be slow to make your mind up in a new relationship but once you're in, you're committed. Your love of a happy home life means you're the perfect match for those who believe home is where the heart is. As an Earth sign you're likely to find your complement in Water signs – Cancer, Scorpio and Pisces. Your dislike of abrupt change makes spontaneous Fire signs – Aries, Leo, Sagittarius – a challenging match for you, whether in love or friendship.

Friends value your faithfulness; a sun-sign Taurus is not and never will be a fair-weather friend. You're by your pal's side, whether you're raising a glass in commiseration or celebration. Your stubborn side can sometimes test the friendship, whether you're picking a place to eat or navigating a disagreement. However, you're not one to give up on a project *or* a person, and your friends know you won't be shaken loose by silly spats. You're ruled by Venus, the relationship planet, and love and harmony wins the day with you.

✦ Rising Sign: Overview ✦

Taurus rising signs translate the patience of a Taurus sun into a serene, unhurried vibe. You take life as it comes, processing challenges with the same unruffled steadiness. Your home is a sanctuary, full of cosy spots where you curl up and find your peace. You prefer to spend time with people who match your calm energy – loud noises make you uncomfortable. However, you are creative and love to collaborate with like-minded souls.

✦ Moon Sign: Overview ✦

Taurus moons take other people's feelings very seriously. You're not one to trifle with emotions or push boundaries. You take people at their word and in return you won't ever tell anyone anything that you don't mean. Your best friend may well be your planner or your spreadsheet and you're in your element when carefully setting foundations for the future. You may be very even-tempered and proud of it but be careful not to let too much resentment build over time. It's better to have a challenging conversation earlier than an explosive argument later.

Ramos Gin Fizz

This recipe is perfect for sensual Taurus suns. It takes a lot of shaking, but results in a striking white, frothy cocktail that's equal parts creamy lightness, citrus zing and botanical gin.

EQUIPMENT

- **Cocktail shaker, filled with ice**
- **Strainer**
- **Old-fashioned glass**

INGREDIENTS

- **50 ml (1⅔ fl oz) gin**
- **30 ml (1 fl oz) lemon juice**
- **30 ml (1 fl oz) lime juice**
- **Dash of simple syrup**
- **Dash of single cream**
- **¼ egg white**
- **3 dashes orange blossom water**
- **Soda to top**

METHOD

Shake all the ingredients but the soda in the cocktail shaker until cocktail is very frothy.

Strain into old-fashioned glass.

Top with soda and enjoy.

Millionaire Mocktail

A non-alcoholic take on the original iconic cocktail. A sweet and citrusy taste of timeless luxury, perfect for Taurus suns who enjoy the finer things in life.

EQUIPMENT

- ✦ Cocktail shaker, filled with ice
- ✦ Strainer
- ✦ Martini glass, chilled

INGREDIENTS

- ✦ 50 ml (1⅔ fl oz) apricot or peach juice
- ✦ 50 ml (1⅔ fl oz) ginger ale
- ✦ 50 ml (1⅔ fl oz) sloe cordial
- ✦ Juice of 1 lime
- ✦ Dash of grenadine
- ✦ Maraschino cherry to garnish

METHOD

Add all ingredients to cocktail shaker and shake until combined.

Strain into a chilled Martini glass and garnish with maraschino cherry.

Sparkling Citrus Punch

Rosemary symbolizes loyalty, one of Taurus's greatest strengths in a relationship. This sparkling punch made with a rosemary syrup is perfect for a Taurus sun to share with a loved one.

EQUIPMENT

+ **Saucepan**
+ **Wooden spoon**
+ **Punchbowl**
+ **Punch glasses**

INGREDIENTS

+ **120 ml (4 fl oz) water**
+ **120 g (4 oz) sugar**
+ **3–6 sprigs rosemary**
+ **750 ml (25½ fl oz) champagne**
+ **120 ml (4 fl oz) grapefruit juice**
+ **120 ml (4 fl oz) orange juice**
+ **30 ml (1 fl oz) grenadine**

METHOD

For the syrup, stir together water, sugar and rosemary in a saucepan and bring to a boil. Lower heat and mix until sugar completely dissolves. Strain and leave to cool.

Combine all the ingredients in a punchbowl.

Chamomile Fizz

Chamomile tea has a calming effect – exactly the vibes that a Taurus rising brings to the table.

EQUIPMENT

- ✦ **Kettle or saucepan**
- ✦ **Cocktail shaker, filled with ice**
- ✦ **Strainer**
- ✦ **Highball glass**

INGREDIENTS

- ✦ **Chamomile teabag**
- ✦ **60 ml (2 fl oz) vodka**
- ✦ **Soda to finish**

METHOD

Brew mug of chamomile tea according to box instructions and leave to cool.

Combine 120 ml (4 fl oz) chamomile tea with vodka in cocktail shaker.

Shake and strain into highball glass filled with ice.

Top with soda to finish.

Vampire

The Vampire needs to be made a day before serving so the flavours infuse – perfect for a forward-thinking Taurus moon.

EQUIPMENT
+ **Cocktail shaker, filled with ice**
+ **Old-fashioned glass**

INGREDIENTS
+ **75 ml (2½ fl oz) tomato juice**
+ **30 ml (1 fl oz) orange juice**
+ **30 ml (1 fl oz) silver tequila**
+ **1 tsp runny honey**
+ **10 ml (⅓ fl oz) lime juice**
+ **1 tsp diced white onion**
+ **½ red chilli, sliced**
+ **Dash of Worcestershire sauce**

METHOD

Combine ingredients in cocktail shaker and shake vigorously.

Strain into container and leave in fridge to combine, overnight.

Serve in old-fashioned glass filled with ice.

Gemini

(21 MAY – 20 JUNE)

RULING PLANET: MERCURY
ELEMENT: AIR

✫ Sun Sign: Overview ✫

A Gemini sun is charm personified. You like to meet people and you never fail to find common ground with your new and future friends. You're very flexible and just as likely to enjoy long, fruity concoctions as you are to sip at punchy, classic cocktails. Friendship isn't the only thing you're adept at – you're a fantastic flirt, too. However, those who know you know that with your sunny nature comes a stormy side. Your sign is the twins and sometimes you wonder if there are two of you trapped inside one body.

PERSONALITY

Although you have your dark side, a Gemini sun much prefers the easy, breezy side of life. You intellectualize emotions where possible, preferring to categorize them rather than engage with them. Information is one of your favourite things – you are one of life's students, always looking to gain fresh knowledge and work out how it fits with what you already know. You're always researching – even when you're set on a course of action, you'll keep plans B and C in your back pocket because you love to have multiple options available.

LOVE AND RELATIONSHIPS

Good communication is the way to your heart. Gemini suns' love thrives on being open and clear about everything, and you mean *everything*. Secrets are your biggest turn off. As far as you're concerned, they block the flow of communication necessary to bring life to a relationship. Your love of information and need to know the "what, where and why" of everything means you can be prone to over-analyze. A suggestion or a gift that you're not expecting can set your mind spinning, so your loved ones need to be patient.

Patience comes into play with your friends and colleagues, too. Your flexibility means you're open to new ideas – but perhaps sometimes too open? Once you've weighed up the pros to so many good ideas, it's hard to know which one to pick, and you become paralyzed by indecision. On the plus side, you're a breath of fresh air. When friends and colleagues ask, "What shall we do?" your answer is, "Try something new!" You're the perfect sounding board – you listen with an open mind, and you've got all the time in the world to bounce ideas back and forth.

✦ Rising Sign: Overview ✦

The Gemini rising is never for lost words when meeting new people. You're straight out the gate with anecdotes and plenty of questions. Remember to take a minute to listen to the answers though, as you can get stuck on transmit sometimes. Your love of analyzing information leads you to have some great observations, and you're always open to sharing them. Like a Gemini sun, you're a great flirt but can be particular about who you settle down with.

✦ Moon Sign: Overview ✦

Gemini moons are witty and quick with a quip. You're always researching new hobbies and new places to explore with friends. Sometimes your quest to find the next best new thing means you don't have time to focus on old interests. However, don't lose your boundless curiosity because it's a light that shines from within. You don't just love learning new things, you love sharing them, too. Your relish for sharing means that your loved ones are always entertained and kept busy.

Slippery Nipple

A layered shooter with two strong sides and a fun, flirty name? Why, a slippery nipple *must* be a Gemini sun! Although the two layers seem different in every way, together they make the perfect match.

EQUIPMENT
+ **Long shot glass**

INGREDIENTS
+ **30 ml (1 fl oz) black sambuca**
+ **30 ml (1 fl oz) Irish cream liqueur**

METHOD

Pour the sambuca into the shot glass.

Carefully layer the Irish cream liqueur on top, keeping the two layers distinct.

Slippery Nipples slide down easy, so best to prepare several for your enjoyment.

Raspberry Martini

Just like Gemini suns, the Martini is a classic cocktail that keeps evolving – so this is practically your mascot drink.

EQUIPMENT

+ **Cocktail shaker**
+ **Strainer**
+ **Martini glass, chilled**

INGREDIENTS

+ **8 raspberries, plus extra for garnish**
+ **120 ml (4 fl oz) gin**
+ **60 ml (2 fl oz) crème de framboise**
+ **10 ml (⅓ fl oz) orange bitters**
+ **Handful of ice**

METHOD

Muddle raspberries in bottom of cocktail shaker.

Add the remaining ingredients and ice and shake until combined and chilled.

Strain into Martini glass and garnish with raspberries.

White Sangria

White Sangria is the perfect sharing summer cocktail – and the perfect way for Gemini suns to attract those who like to put their toe outside of the everyday.

EQUIPMENT

- ✦ Jug
- ✦ Wine glass
- ✦ Muddler or wooden spoon

INGREDIENTS

- ✦ Juice of 1 lemon
- ✦ 1 lemon, sliced
- ✦ 1 lime, sliced
- ✦ 2 apples, cored and sliced
- ✦ 150 g (5⅓ oz) white sugar
- ✦ 750 ml (25½ fl oz) white wine, chilled
- ✦ 60 ml (2 fl oz) brandy
- ✦ 500 ml (19 fl oz) ginger ale

METHOD

Add fruit and lemon juice to the pitcher.

Add sugar and mix until dissolved

Pour the wine and brandy over the ingredients, mixing until fully combined.

Gently stir in ginger ale.

Zingy Virgin Strawberry Daiquiri

Like a Gemini rising sign, daiquiris add sparkle to any situation. This mocktail relies a little less on the traditional art of cocktail-making and more on the modern art of the kitchen blender.

EQUIPMENT
+ **Blender**

INGREDIENTS
+ **4 medium strawberries, hulled**
+ **50 g (1⅔ oz) white sugar**
+ **1 tbsp lemon juice**
+ **200 ml (6⅔ fl oz) lemon and lime soda**
+ **Handful of ice cubes**
+ **Welled margarita glass**

METHOD

Pulse together all the ingredients except the ice, until combined.

Add ice and blend on medium speed until combined.

Honey Bee

Gemini moons are as busy as a bee, so they should treat themselves to a little sip of honey every now and then.

EQUIPMENT

- ✦ **Cocktail shaker**
- ✦ **Bar spoon**
- ✦ **Strainer**
- ✦ **Martini glass**

INGREDIENTS

- ✦ **60 ml (2 fl oz) white rum**
- ✦ **2 tbsp runny honey**
- ✦ **40 ml (1⅓ fl oz) lemon juice**
- ✦ **Handful of ice**

METHOD

Add the rum and honey to a cocktail shaker and stir.

Add ice and lemon juice and shake until combined and chilled.

Strain into the Martini glass.

Enjoy the sweet nectar!

Cancer

(21 JUNE – 22 JULY)

RULING PLANET: MOON
ELEMENT: WATER

✦ Sun Sign: Overview ✦

It's fitting that the animal for Cancerians is a crab, because you sure are softies on the inside. There are boundless feelings hidden behind that shell of yours. Although strangers may think they've met someone reserved, even a bit tough, your loved ones are very well acquainted with your (sometimes overflowing) emotions. Once someone has found their way into your heart, they're there for keeps. And that goes for objects too! Besties? For life. Favourite cocktails? For ever.

PERSONALITY

Having all those emotions can be useful because you have a deep emotional intelligence and you can read the room like no other. You put those skills to good use, going out of your way to make sure everyone around you is comfortable and content. Your love is powerful but be careful to not let it become overpowering; Sun-sign Cancerians suffer from possessive tendencies and must nip those in the bud when they can. Like any water sign, you are blessed with creativity and an active imagination; there are magical worlds inside your head that you're ready to share with your loved ones.

LOVE AND RELATIONSHIPS

If music be the food of love, then the sun-sign Cancerian's favourite tune is a beautiful harmony. You don't enjoy the loud clash of a tempestuous relationship; you prefer the sound of voices singing in perfect chorus. You look for shared interests and seek out shared values in both platonic and romantic relationships. When the good ship Cancerian navigates romantic waters, you are looking for a safe port: somewhere to drop anchor and build something that will stand the test of time.

When it comes to friends, a sun-sign Cancerian always has arms ready for hugging, snacks stored in the cupboard and a listening ear. You'll be there to listen to your friend's woes long after others have tired of the subject. However, despite how comfortable you are sharing your surface feelings, you tend to hold back when it comes to your deeper emotions. You should be more confident in sharing your heart with friends; it will lighten your burdens and your friends will appreciate being taken into your confidence. They trust you with their vulnerabilities, so maybe it's time for you to return their trust.

⋆⋆ Rising Sign: Overview ⋆⋆

A rising-sign Cancerian's best friend is time. You need a minute to process the situation and generate the "right" reaction. You don't love attempting to problem-solve in the heat of the moment, but prefer to take the problem away, mull it over and return with a resolution. You are the same in new situations or with new people, but once you get to know someone you blossom. Your friends are chosen family, and while you won't start a fight, you'll rally to the cause when your loved ones are threatened.

⋆⋆ Moon Sign: Overview ⋆⋆

Cancer moons aren't afraid of deep feelings – in fact, you embrace them. A river runs deep within you, and you will travel its course. Remember that, like a river, you're always flowing and changing. Sometimes you hold on so tightly to your needs and desires that you forget to allow yourself room for growth. Stop and check in with yourself: what do you really want? You consider yourself responsible for others' emotional well-being and your nurturing nature means you'll take the utmost care of them.

Aviation

Sun-sign Cancerians love the classics, and you don't get much more classic than this violet-hued cocktail invented at the turn of the twentieth century.

EQUIPMENT
+ **Cocktail shaker, filled with ice**
+ **Strainer**
+ **Coupe glass, chilled**

INGREDIENTS
+ **120 ml (4 fl oz) gin**
+ **30 ml (1 fl oz) freshly squeezed lemon juice**
+ **30 ml (1 fl oz) maraschino liqueur**
+ **30 ml (1 fl oz) crème de violette**

METHOD

Add all the ingredients to the cocktail shaker and shake until combined.

Strain into coupe glass.

Enjoy how the light plays in the violet hues (if you can resist drinking this delicious concoction too quickly).

Limonada Suíça

Lemonade made using limes and containing cream – this unique non-alcoholic recipe is perfect for the sun-sign Cancerian.

EQUIPMENT

- ✦ **Blender**
- ✦ **Highball glass, chilled**
- ✦ **Sieve**
- ✦ **Jug, chilled**

INGREDIENTS

- ✦ **4 limes**
- ✦ **400 ml (13⅔ fl oz) sweetened condensed milk**
- ✦ **950 ml (32 fl oz) water**
- ✦ **Handful of ice**

METHOD

Peel two of your limes, remove the pith.

Cut all limes into wedges and pulse with water in blender until combined

Strain through sieve, retaining only the liquid

Combine in blender with condensed milk and ice, blending until frothy and ice-cool, before pouring into a jug.

Pimm's Cup

Cancer suns believe that sharing is caring, and they care, a lot. And what could be better than a Pimm's jug for Cancerians to share with friends?

EQUIPMENT
+ **Jug**
+ **Large wooden spoon**

INGREDIENTS
+ **½ cucumber, sliced into rounds**
+ **5 strawberries, halved**
+ **Oranges, cut into wedges**
+ **Handful of mint leaves, bruised**
+ **250 ml (8½ fl oz) Pimm's No 1**
+ **550 ml (18½ fl oz) lemonade, chilled**

METHOD

Lightly muddle the fruit, mint and Pimm's in the jug.

Top with lemonade and stir.

This recipe is all about flexibility – reduce the amount of Pimm's for a light daytime drink or hold back on the lemonade for a stronger concoction.

Kir Royale

The original Kir Royale was named after World War Two freedom fighter Felix Kir. Like Kir, Cancer rising signs will rally to a cause when called to it.

EQUIPMENT

+ **Champagne flute**

INGREDIENTS

+ **15 ml (½ fl oz) crème de cassis**
+ **Champagne, chilled, to top**
+ **2 frozen blackberries**

METHOD

Add the crème de cassis to the flute and top with champagne.

Garnish with frozen blackberries.

You can use fresh fruit for this recipe, but the frozen blackberries will help the cocktail remain chilled for longer.

Old Pal

The Old Pal is a classic cocktail consisting of punchy spirits with just enough Campari to sweeten the flavour. It's the perfect cocktail for the moon-sign Cancerian whose tastes are ever-evolving.

EQUIPMENT
+ **Cocktail shaker, filled with ice**
+ **Strainer**
+ **Old-fashioned glass, filled with ice**

INGREDIENTS
+ **60 ml (2 fl oz) bourbon**
+ **60 ml (2 fl oz) dry vermouth**
+ **60 ml (2 fl oz) red amaro**

METHOD
Combine the ingredients in the cocktail shaker.

Shake until combined and strain into old-fashioned glass.

Bottoms up!

Leo

(23 JULY – 22 AUGUST)

**RULING PLANET: SUN
ELEMENT: FIRE**

⋆ Sun Sign: Overview ⋆

The Leo's ruling planet is the sun. How apt! Your charisma pulls people into your orbit and means that you are often the centre of attention. In fact, sometimes you crave it, and you may indulge yourself by shaking things up and generating some drama for your own amusement. You mean no harm – a flamboyant cocktail here, a controversial opinion there – but the resulting kerfuffle isn't welcomed by all. Still, your powerful magnetism means ruffled feelings are soon soothed.

PERSONALITY

As a sun-sign Leo, you fancy yourself a leader, and you have lots of qualities that make you right for those roles. You inspire others to follow in your path, and you always have passion and enthusiasm for the task at hand. However, you're not as invulnerable as the image you project. Your feelings can be easily hurt at even the most kindly meant critique. Your creative force powers both your imaginative approach to life and your sometimes flamboyant self-expression. Sun-sign Leos are also blessed with that quality rarely found in creatives – organization!

LOVE AND RELATIONSHIPS

Being the object of a sun-sign Leo's affection is like standing in a sunbeam; it warms you to your soul. You give so much of yourself to friends and loved ones and go to great lengths to make them happy. However, such powerful affection can't sustain itself. You need to be sure your love is reciprocated or else your flame sputters.

There's only room for one person in the centre of your friendship group's attention and that's you! Still, that doesn't mean you prefer shy wallflowers in your inner circle. Sun-sign Leos mesh well with fast-paced, confident air signs such as Gemini, Libra and Aquarius, who can keep up with your hijinks. Sometimes, what you consider to be your take-charge attitude tips over into bossiness, so be careful of when you are taking control of plans and when you are dominating them. You're an optimist and that's a quality you bring to your personal and professional relationships. Just when the mood flags and everyone's energy dips, your sunny disposition is here to save the day.

✦ Rising Sign: Overview ✦

A rising-sign Leo is a born entertainer. You have a big character and you use your flair for the dramatic for the benefit of your audience. Has a rising-sign Leo ever been intimidated by being in a new situation? Rarely! For you it's an opportunity to take control and take the lead. Yes, you have an ego but your penchant for leadership roles means you put it to good use. You enjoy being admired – but sometimes so much so that you fall into the trap of people-pleasing.

✦ Moon Sign: Overview ✦

A moon-sign Leo relishes the dramatic – and the melodramatic. If there are no emotional events to be found then you don't mind creating some. A little push here, a little pull there and voilà! Plenty of excitement taking place with you in the centre of it all. You love to love, and friends and loved ones can find themselves showered with physical affection and gifts. Like the moon reflects the sun, a moon-sign Leo flourishes when their love is shone back at them. Your intensity is diffused by your charm and tremendous sense of humour.

Turmeric and Ginger Shooter

If a Leo sun's energy and warmth could be distilled into a non-alcoholic shooter, it would be this one. The citrus and ginger have the zip of a Leo on the go, while the turmeric adds a gentle warmth that you bring to the room.

EQUIPMENT

+ **Blender**
+ **Wooden spoon**
+ **Long shot glass**
+ **Fine-mesh strainer**
+ **Cocktail shaker, filled with ice**

INGREDIENTS

+ **Juice of 1 orange**
+ **Juice of 2 lemons**
+ **30 g (1 oz) fresh turmeric, chopped**
+ **30 g (1 oz) fresh ginger, peeled and chopped**

METHOD

Whizz ingredients together in a blender on the highest speed.

Shake mixture in the cocktail shaker to chill.

Strain into the shot glass through a fine-mesh strainer, pressing pulp with a wooden spoon to maximize the flavour.

Showbiz

The Showbiz is wonderfully eye-catching, with a striking dark-purple hue created by the crème de cassis, perfect for the party-loving Leo sun.

EQUIPMENT

+ **Cocktail shaker, filled with ice**
+ **Martini glass, chilled**
+ **Strainer**
+ **Cocktail stick, to serve**

INGREDIENTS

+ **60 ml (2 fl oz) vodka**
+ **30 ml (1 fl oz) crème de cassis**
+ **60 ml (2 fl oz) grapefruit juice**
+ **Fresh blackberries to serve**

METHOD

Combine the liquid ingredients in a cocktail shaker.

Shake to combine and strain into Martini glass.

Skewer three blackberries on a cocktail stick and balance on rim of the glass.

Serving suggestion: swan around sipping from this cocktail saying, "that's showbiz for you."

Lotus Blossom

Champagne and sake are two bold alcohols with their own unique flavours and histories. And yet, they work so well together – Leo suns can drink this and learn that compromise isn't so scary after all.

EQUIPMENT

+ **Cocktail shaker, filled with ice**
+ **Strainer**
+ **Old-fashioned glass**

INGREDIENTS

+ **60 ml (2 fl oz) vodka**
+ **60 ml (2 fl oz) lychee juice**
+ **30 ml (1 fl oz) sake**

METHOD

Add the vodka, sake and lychee juice to the cocktail shaker and shake until combined.

Strain into glass.

Top tip: lychee juice can be swapped for lychee syrup, depending on availability in your area.

Brandy Alexander

Is a Brandy Alexander a cocktail or is it dessert? Who cares? It's delicious *and* it's a talking point – and a Leo rising sign loves to make a stir.

EQUIPMENT

+ **Cocktail shaker, filled with ice**
+ **Strainer**
+ **Old-fashioned glass, chilled**

INGREDIENTS

+ **50 ml (1⅔ fl oz) brandy**
+ **30 ml (1 fl oz) white crème de cacao**
+ **30 ml (1 fl oz) dark crème de cacao**
+ **30 ml (1 fl oz) double cream**
+ **30 ml (1 fl oz) whole milk**
+ **Pinch ground nutmeg, to garnish**

METHOD

Shake liquid ingredients together in cocktail shaker, just long enough to combine and chill.

Strain into glass and sprinkle a pinch of nutmeg over the top.

Corpse Reviver No.1

Is the name a touch melodramatic? Perhaps... But that's just like a moon-sign Leo.

EQUIPMENT

+ **Cocktail shaker, filled with ice**
+ **Bar spoon**
+ **Strainer**
+ **Martini glass**

INGREDIENTS

+ **60 ml (2 fl oz) brandy**
+ **60 ml (2 fl oz) apple brandy**
+ **60 ml (2 fl oz) sweet vermouth**

METHOD

Mix together the ingredients in a cocktail shaker – this is stirred, not shaken.

Strain into the Martini glass.

A larger-than-life cocktail for a larger-than-life Leo.

Virgo
(23 AUGUST – 22 SEPTEMBER)

RULING PLANET: MERCURY
ELEMENT: EARTH

✦ Sun Sign: Overview ✦

The sun-sign Virgo's symbol is a maiden but it could just as fittingly be a bee. Always buzzing through your never-ending to-do list and helping others, you're as busy as a whole hive! Your approach is meticulous, from life admin to cocktail-making. But your desire for perfection means you can subject yourself to intense critique. You think it's a valuable part of any process, so you are surprised when others don't welcome the same scrutiny.

PERSONALITY

For all that you enjoy helping others, you don't seek adulation or praise in return. In fact, it turns you off completely. As one of the humblest sun signs, you see far more use in critiquing your process to improve it for next time than spending time patting yourself on the back. If you can stand to hear some praise, then know that you're thoughtful, kind and all-in on your passions. Your dedication can tip over into obsessiveness – remember that even you need some time to relax and that you deserve a little dose of your own kindness.

LOVE AND RELATIONSHIPS

Love transforms a sun-sign Virgo's care and attention into patient kindness. You're very thoughtful and your attention to detail means that you pick up on loved ones' wants. In fact, you meet needs that your loved ones didn't even realize they had. You're not such a fan of the spontaneous side of love – you prefer to be the captain of your love boat. However, you can't micromanage falling in love. You come into your own in established relationships as your focus means you rarely let the relationship fall by the wayside.

Your friendships flourish with people whose opinions of themselves aren't easily dented. Those with inflated self-perception may feel the prick of your observations too sharply. Calm, resilient water signs such as Cancer, Scorpio and Pisces suit you best: your grounded nature provides a safe presence that they value, and they don't mind the time that you spend buried in analysis.

✦ Rising Sign: Overview ✦

Virgo rising signs are masters of practical magic. You can transform what appears to be chaos into order. Your strategy is always to simplify, and if it's not workable, then you're not interested! Virgo rising signs love to help others. You're not just a problem solver, you're a healer, too. It might help you to remind yourself that you deserve to receive just as much care as you give to others. Don't deny yourself the help you'd happily give others – you deserve it, too.

✦ Moon Sign: Overview ✦

An ordered life is a happy life for a moon-sign Virgo. Once you've arranged your life to your liking, you believe everything should run like clockwork. You take pleasure in the process. Luckily for you, this gives you the superpower of enjoying chores and errands! It's the tricky emotional stuff that trips you up. You're open to love but the lid on your emotions doesn't come off lightly. First a sliver, then a wedge, until finally the door is open and you can express your deeply felt emotions.

Mojito

This cocktail recipe requires Virgo suns to apply their usual meticulous approach. The ingredients list is simple; it's the process that makes the flavours sing.

EQUIPMENT

+ **Cocktail shaker**
+ **Muddler**
+ **Highball glass, filled with ice**

INGREDIENTS

+ **1 lime, halved**
+ **Four mint leaves**
+ **1 tsp granulated sugar**
+ **60 ml (2 fl oz) white rum**
+ **Soda, to top**

METHOD

Remove pips and squeeze juice of one lime over mint leaves and sugar in a cocktail shaker.

Muddle together until mint leaves are bruised.

Transfer mixture into glass.

Pour rum over the ice and ingredients and gently stir together.

Top with soda.

Batida de Coco

This recipe is so delicious that even a Virgo sun sign can find no fault with it. It's a creamy, tropical concoction to be enjoyed in summer.

EQUIPMENT
+ **Blender**
+ **Highball glass, filled with ice**

INGREDIENTS
+ **Desiccated coconut, to garnish (optional)**
+ **120 ml (4 fl oz) cachaça**
+ **90 ml (3 fl oz) cream of coconut**
+ **60 ml (2 fl oz) coconut milk**
+ **2 ice cubes**

METHOD

If garnishing, pour the desiccated coconut onto a small plate. Wet the rim of the glass and roll in the coconut to create a take on the margarita-style rim.

Blitz together the remaining ingredients in a blender on the highest speed.

Pour your cocktail and enjoy while imagining a tropical paradise.

Fog Cutter

A Virgo sun is always looking to cut through the nonsense, albeit kindly. A Fog Cutter adds a dash of citrus to soften its blow. Use this cocktail to help you use your words to your best advantage.

EQUIPMENT

+ **Cocktail shaker, filled with ice**
+ **Strainer**
+ **Highball glass, filled with ice**

INGREDIENTS

+ **60 ml (2 fl oz) rum**
+ **30 ml (1 fl oz) gin**
+ **30 ml (1 fl oz) lemon juice, freshly squeezed**
+ **30 ml (1 fl oz) cognac**
+ **120 ml (4 fl oz) orange juice, freshly squeezed**

METHOD

Combine ingredients in cocktail shaker and shake well.

Strain into highball.

Brace yourself, because this sharp cocktail is coming at you straight out the glass.

Limoncello Thyme

Virgo rising signs are healers, and this limoncello-gin cocktail, enriched with decongesting thyme, is your perfect tonic.

EQUIPMENT

- ✦ **Cocktail shaker, with ice to add**
- ✦ **Muddler**
- ✦ **Strainer**
- ✦ **Highball glass, filled with ice**

INGREDIENTS

- ✦ **3 sprigs thyme**
- ✦ **60 ml (2 fl oz) gin**
- ✦ **30 ml (1 fl oz) limoncello**
- ✦ **30 ml (1 fl oz) lime juice, freshly squeezed**
- ✦ **Soda water, to top**

METHOD

Muddle two sprigs of thyme in the base of the cocktail shaker, then add the ice.

Pour in gin, limoncello and lime juice and shake thoroughly.

Strain into a highball glass and top with soda water.

Garnish with one sprig of thyme.

Arnold Palmer

This non-alcoholic iced-tea and lemonade combination is the perfect refreshing summer drink. It does take some planning ahead to prepare the tea, which a moon sign Virgo is more than equal to.

EQUIPMENT
+ **Highball glass, filled with ice**
+ **Bar spoon**

INGREDIENTS
+ **150 ml (5 fl oz) iced tea**
+ **100 ml (3⅓ fl oz) lemonade**
+ **Lemon round, to garnish**

METHOD

Pour tea and lemonade into glass and stir gently to combine without deflating the lemonade. For a dramatic layered effect, first pour cloudy lemonade and then gently top with iced tea without stirring.

Cut halfway into the lemon round and slide it onto the rim of your glass for a sunshine garnish.

Libra

(23 SEPTEMBER – 22 OCTOBER)

RULING PLANET: VENUS
ELEMENT: AIR

⋆ ⋆ Sun Sign: Overview ⋆ ⋆

Sun-sign Libra's natural habitat is surrounded by friends. You not only enjoy others' company but grow from exposure to their ideas. You welcome new opinions and concepts and you're always willing to look at life from other people's perspectives. In fact, you need strong voices in your life. When left to your own devices you tend to hesitate on your decisions, always talking yourself in to and then back out of a conclusion. Your openness to a variety of points of view makes you the perfect diplomat.

PERSONALITY

Sun-sign Libras have all the personality traits that make you enjoyable company. You are easy-going, fun-loving and affectionate. You spend so much time around people that you're an expert at reading the room. You're able to quickly suss out people who lie or are insincere and you have no time for them. Why would you, when you could be enjoying good times with friends? Your indecisiveness can lead to hastiness, choosing something because you feel pressured to do so rather than because you think it's the right decision.

LOVE AND RELATIONSHIPS

Sun-sign Libras are easy going in friendship but choosy when it comes to love. You have strong ideals, which can lead to high expectations that bring disappointment. But that's ok, as you're not always looking for a long-lasting relationship or love connection. Earth signs such as Taurus might not be in harmony with this air-sign behaviour so be careful whose heart you tangle with.

Your peacemaker tendencies make you a valued member of any friendship team. No matter how high tempers flare or how polarized your friends' perspectives are, you can find a way to bridge the gap and restore peace. However, don't forget that not all conflict is unhealthy. Unaired feelings can lead to resentment – it is not fair to punish your loved ones if they don't know what they've done wrong.

While sun-sign Libras are expert friends and caring lovers, there's one relationship that could use a little more work. You might cringe but yes... it's your relationship with yourself. You're fabulous company! You can find pleasure in solitude if you let go of your anxiety surrounding being on your own.

⋆✦ Rising Sign: Overview ⋆✦

When a rising-sign Libra sets about solving a problem, you ask yourself one question: what's the fairest solution? You take pleasure from harmony in all things. This means you will put time and care into making your surroundings as lovely to you as possible. Your desire to always be diplomatic can be mistaken for a lack of backbone. You are so busy ensuring everyone is happy that others are left wondering if you know what you yourself want.

⋆✦ Moon Sign: Overview ✦⋆

A moon-sign Libra is a real scholar of people. You love to hear new opinions and you'll use them as a basis to build your worldview. You read the room with such speed that you often react to situations based on what others are feeling before you consider your own perspective. This can disconcert some people, who worry that you're sidelining your own wants and needs for the sake of others. However, you are emotionally fulfilled by your connection with the people in your life, whether that's your family, friends, loved ones or colleagues.

Sea Breeze

Sun-sign Libras are easy breezy, and so is this cocktail. The grapefruit juice is best when freshly squeezed as the fruit's famous sharpness adds a necessary lift to the flavour.

EQUIPMENT

+ **Cocktail shaker, filled with ice**
+ **Strainer**
+ **Old-fashioned glass, chilled**

INGREDIENTS

+ **60 ml (2 fl oz) vodka**
+ **100 ml (3⅓ fl oz) cranberry juice**
+ **30 ml (1 fl oz) grapefruit juice, freshly squeezed**
+ **Lime wedge, to garnish**

METHOD

Shake all the liquid ingredients together in the cocktail shaker.

Strain into an old-fashioned glass and garnish with a lime wedge.

Optional: shake extra hard to give the top of the cocktail an appearance of foam, as if it were a wave whipped up by the wind.

Long Island Iced Tea

Libra suns may sometimes struggle to make decisions. Are you in the mood for tequila or rum, gin or vodka? With the Long Island iced tea, there's no need to pick – it's all in there!

EQUIPMENT
+ **Highball glass, filled with ice**
+ **Bar spoon**

INGREDIENTS
+ **15 ml (½ fl oz) tequila**
+ **15 ml (½ fl oz) vodka**
+ **15 ml (½ fl oz) white rum**
+ **15 ml (½ fl oz) Cointreau**
+ **15 ml (½ fl oz) gin**
+ **30 ml (1 fl oz) lemon juice**
+ **20 ml (⅔ fl oz) simple syrup**
+ **Cola, to top**

METHOD

Add all the ingredients to the glass and gently stir to combine.

Top with the cola.

Brace yourself!

Pink Gin Iced Tea

Just like Libra suns bring peace to their loved ones, this calming chamomile will bring peace to your soul.

EQUIPMENT

+ **Jug, filled with ice**
+ **Bar spoon**
+ **2 highball glasses, for serving**

INGREDIENTS

+ **500 ml (19 fl oz) hot water, boiled**
+ **1 chamomile tea bag**
+ **100 ml (3⅓ fl oz) pink gin**
+ **100 ml (3⅓ fl oz) spiced rum**
+ **100 ml (3⅓ fl oz) elderflower cordial**
+ **100 ml (3⅓ fl oz) lychee juice**
+ **Handful of ice**
+ **Chamomile flowers, to garnish**

METHOD

In the jug, steep teabag in hot water for 5 minutes, remove bag and leave liquid to cool.

When at room temperature, add the remaining ingredients and stir with bar spoon.

Add ice to cool further and garnish with flowers.

Diplomat

This recipe is perfect for the natural diplomat Libra rising sign. The cocktail was allegedly popular in the French diplomatic service in the early-twentieth century.

EQUIPMENT
+ **Cocktail shaker, filled with ice**
+ **Strainer**
+ **Martini glass, chilled**

INGREDIENTS
+ **120 ml (4 fl oz) dry vermouth**
+ **120 ml (4 fl oz) sweet vermouth**
+ **Dash maraschino**
+ **Twist of orange peel, to garnish**

METHOD

Stir the liquid ingredients gently in the cocktail shaker. Shaking the mixture can froth and cloud the vermouth – this cocktail looks most inviting in its original clear amber.

Strain into the Martini glass and garnish with a twist of orange peel.

Frozen Watermelon Margarita

Like a Libra moon sign, this frozen watermelon Margarita is a real people pleaser. It's non-alcoholic, too, which means you can enjoy it from sunup to sundown.

EQUIPMENT

- ✦ Blender
- ✦ Fine-mesh sieve
- ✦ Cocktail shaker
- ✦ Muddler
- ✦ Strainer
- ✦ Margarita glass, chilled

INGREDIENTS

- ✦ 200 g (7 oz) frozen watermelon, cubed
- ✦ 1 tbsp sugar
- ✦ Wedge of lime
- ✦ Handful mint leaves, plus sprig to garnish
- ✦ Sparkling water to top

METHOD

Blitz watermelon in a blender on the highest speed and sieve into glass.

Muddle sugar, mint and lime in a jug until lime has released juices.

Stir in watermelon juice and strain into margarita glass.

Gently top with sparkling water and garnish with mint.

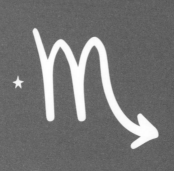

Scorpio

(23 OCTOBER – 21 NOVEMBER)

RULING PLANET: PLUTO
ELEMENT: WATER

⁺✦ Sun Sign: Overview ⁺✦

Rivers run deep in passionate water-sign Scorpio. You pull from a vast well of emotion and those who encounter you are just as likely to be swept up in your coursing energy. You put all that power and energy to good use – have you encountered a challenge? Bring it on! You have imagination and willpower on your side. But, at times, you can be a little possessive. What's yours is yours – you internally groan when someone suggests splitting a jug of cocktails – and you're not a big fan of sharing.

PERSONALITY

Passion is the name of your game. You care – *a lot*! That's good news for your loved ones, your hobbies and your career, all of which can flourish under your seemingly limitless attention. Unfortunately, you don't discriminate between positive and negative objects of your attention, which can lead to frustrations developing into grudges and obsessions. You have a strong sense of self and you're frank with yourself about your strengths and weaknesses. This gives you an advantage when assessing others; you see through insincerity and flimflam with ease.

LOVE AND RELATIONSHIPS

Sun-sign Scorpios have a reputation as the most amorous sign. However, you're all about quality, not quantity. It's the meaningful connections for you. Your relationships must start with a spark and from there it's a slow burn, stoking the flames into a powerful blaze. Like fire, your love can burn the not-careful. Your loved one is the centre of your world and you would like to be the centre of theirs. This means you are on the lookout for rivals for their attention and may start to spot things that aren't there.

On meeting new people, sun-sign Scorpios are more likely to scope out competitors and rivals before spying future friends. Still, once someone has gained your trust and affection, they have a loyal friend till the end of their days. Everything you do is purposeful, so you have little time for flighty and dreamy air signs. Instead, you prefer to ally with people who can help put your plans into motion, with a practical eye and a flair for planning.

⋆★ Rising Sign: Overview ★⋆

Scorpio rising signs are fizzing with energy – but that's
OK because you always know what to do with it, right?
Others might be intimidated by your intensity of feeling
but you use it to fuel your drive. Unfortunately, you
extend that same energy to maintaining the protective
shell around your inner feelings. You fear that letting
people in will leave you open to weakness. But, once
you use that Scorpio rising bravery to battle your fears,
you are a wonderful friend.

⋆★ Moon Sign: Overview ★⋆

Just as there are two sides to the moon, there are two
sides to moon-sign Scorpios. You have all that Scorpio
emotion running through your veins but you keep it
tightly under wraps. Your fear of appearing vulnerable
means you shut yourself off from what can be a
beautiful and powerful relationship. Once you open up,
you bring your considerable strength to the relationship,
taking all the loyalty and love that's given to you and
returning it with all that you have. Remember: you can
find strength in your vulnerability.

El Diablo

Scorpio suns have the reputation of being intense and passionate, so why not play with that a little with this cocktail, which shares its name with the devil himself.

EQUIPMENT

- ✦ **Cocktail shaker, filled with ice**
- ✦ **Strainer**
- ✦ **Highball glass, filled with ice**

INGREDIENTS

- ✦ **90 ml (3 fl oz) tequila**
- ✦ **20 ml (⅔ fl oz) crème de cassis**
- ✦ **60 ml (2 fl oz) lime juice, freshly squeezed**
- ✦ **Ginger beer, to top**

METHOD

Shake the alcohol and lime juice together in a cocktail shaker.

Strain into a glass.

Gently top with ginger beer.

Kombucha Mule

While the kick in a Moscow Mule comes from the vodka, in the non-alcoholic Kombucha Mule, the kombucha, a mildly fermented drink, carries the stinger.

EQUIPMENT
+ **Highball glass, filled with ice**

INGREDIENTS
+ **30 ml (1 fl oz) lime juice, freshly squeezed**
+ **Ginger-flavoured kombucha, to top**
+ **Sprig of mint, to garnish**

METHOD

Add the lime juice to the glass and gently pour over with kombucha.

Garnish with sprig of mint.

Serving suggestion: serve in a copper mug, the traditional Moscow Mule vessel.

Ginger Snap

The warmth of this fiery cocktail gives you the same tingle as the first stirrings of attraction. This should give any Scorpio sun the fuel they need to pursue their passions.

EQUIPMENT

+ **Cocktail shaker, filled with ice**
+ **Strainer**
+ **Coupe glass**

INGREDIENTS

+ **30 ml (1 fl oz) scotch**
+ **15 ml (½ fl oz) gin**
+ **Dash Angostura bitters**
+ **15 ml (½ fl oz) ginger liqueur**
+ **15 ml (½ fl oz) lemon juice**
+ **Ginger beer, to top**

METHOD

Shake ingredients, except the ginger beer, together in cocktail shaker.

Strain into coupe glass and top with ginger beer.

Serve on a cold night in front of a warm fire, with a special someone.

Queimada

This fiery Galician cocktail is perfect for the daring Scorpio rising sign.

EQUIPMENT

+ **Clay pot**
+ **Ladle**
+ **Gloves**
+ **Long matches or candle lighter**
+ **Mugs**

INGREDIENTS

+ **70 g (2½ oz) granulated sugar**
+ **75 g (2⅔ oz) coffee beans**
+ **Apples, chopped**
+ **1 litre orujo (35 fl oz) (or grappa above 50 per cent proof)**
+ **Rind of one lemon or orange**

METHOD

In a separate container, mix 10 g (⅓ oz) of sugar and a ladleful of orujo until the sugar dissolves.

Add the remaining ingredients to the clay pot and set in a safe place.

Wearing gloves as a precaution, set the mixture alight.

Using the ladle, pour the reserved sugar and orujo over the mixture.

Ladle a mix of the delicious liquid and fruit into mugs.

Cranberry Bourbon Smash

The dual nature of this cocktail evokes the Scorpio moon's two sides; the juices flirt with the fruitier layers and disguise the punchier spirit flavours.

EQUIPMENT

- Muddler
- Cocktail shaker, with ice to add
- Strainer
- Highball glass, chilled

INGREDIENTS

- 10 raspberries
- 180 ml (6 fl oz) cranberry juice
- 60 ml (2 fl oz) lime juice
- 120 ml (4 fl oz) bourbon
- 15 ml (½ fl oz) sugar syrup
- Dash Angostura bitters
- Sprig mint leaves, to garnish

METHOD

Muddle raspberries at the bottom of the shaker.

Add liquid ingredients and ice, shaking well to combine before straining into a chilled glass.

Lightly bruise mint for flavour release by smacking gently against your palm, and add to glass.

Sagittarius
(22 NOVEMBER – 21 DECEMBER)

RULING PLANET: JUPITER
ELEMENT: FIRE

✦ Sun Sign: Overview ✦

As a fearless sun-sign Sagittarian, you love to say yes to adventure. You'll keep roving as long as the horizon is still in your sights, pursuing your next new experience with enthusiasm. As might be expected from an explorer, you are broad-minded and admire that quality in others. Rules and regulations are the only things that truly scare you – you can't stand the feeling of being caged by them. This aversion can tip your impulsive nature into recklessness as you'll say "no" to a regulation before you ask, "why"?

PERSONALITY

A sun-sign Sagittarian breezes into any room and spreads their cheer and enthusiasm to anyone they encounter. Although you enjoy meeting new people and have great respect for your friends and loved ones, you're very independent. Given your constant movement and progression, you don't have much time for staying still and really delving into something – whether that's a project or a relationship. This can lead friends to feel that you can be unemotional or closed off sometimes.

LOVE AND RELATIONSHIPS

Sagittarians are pretty good at writing a dating bio. You love adventure, you've got plenty of ambition and masses of energy and you possess a natural curiosity about the world. Short-term partners can guarantee that any date with you will leave them with a smile and a good story to tell. Long-term partners tend to have more on their plate. Your default suspicion is that the grass is greener on the other side and you're quite willing to peep over the fence to find out.

You've got a long contact list, plenty of connections on social media and you're a great resource for pals with a query or a need. However, the deeper connections sometimes elude you and, in the rare moments you stop to take a breath, you might feel a little bit lonely. Birthday cards and weekly hangouts aren't your speciality but once-in-a-lifetime adventures are. Plus, it doesn't matter to you whether it's been a week or a year since you last saw a friend, you're just as pleased to see them.

⭐ Rising Sign: Overview ⭐

Sagittarian rising signs prize experiences over material possessions. You'd rather sleep under a canopy of stars than of silk. Bumps in the road don't intimidate you and your infectious enthusiasm can sweep others along for the adventure, too. But not everyone agrees with your belief that life is a game; grounded earth signs might find themselves tripped up by your agile, merry outlook on life. Your big personality appears larger than life and you shine in any social situation.

⭐ Moon Sign: Overview ⭐

Moon-sign Sagittarians embody the belief that every journey starts with the first step. By avoiding getting bogged down in doubts before you've even started, you go farther than most. Such enthusiasm and optimism has a positive impact on those around you, inspiring them to act, too. Your desire to keep moving feeds into a near-fear of stagnation. You'll leave – whether that's a job, a hobby or relationship – before you find yourself in a rut. In certain lights, moving on to new pastures can look a lot like running away from your troubles.

Midnight Stinger

The Midnight Stinger injects a bit of pizzazz into any situation, just like a Sagittarius sun injects life into any room they're in.

EQUIPMENT

- **Cocktail shaker, filled with ice**
- **Strainer**
- **Old-fashioned glass, filled with ice**

INGREDIENTS

- **30 ml (1 fl oz) bourbon**
- **30 ml (1 fl oz) Branca Menta**
- **30 ml (1 fl oz) lemon juice, freshly squeezed**
- **Sprig mint leaves, to garnish**

METHOD

Shake the liquid ingredients together in cocktail shaker. Strain into old-fashioned glass.

Lightly bruise mint leaves by smacking them against your palm and then place in glass.

Tokyo Bloody Mary

Just like a Sagittarius sun, this cocktail is worldly, taking inspiration from all over the globe. The traditional vodka is replaced by sake in this take on the classic.

EQUIPMENT

- **Cocktail shaker, filled with ice**
- **Strainer**
- **Highball glass, chilled**

INGREDIENTS

- **60 ml (2 fl oz) sake**
- **240 ml (8 fl oz) tomato juice**
- **15 ml (½ fl oz) lemon juice**
- **8 dashes Tabasco sauce**
- **8 dashes Worcestershire sauce**
- **Pinch celery salt**
- **Pinch black pepper**
- **Celery stalk, to serve**

METHOD

Combine all the ingredients except the celery stalk in a cocktail shaker.

Shake firmly and strain into a highball glass.

Garnish with stick of celery.

Apple Pie

This spicy number can bring the heat a Sagittarius sun needs to their relationships. When served hot, it's the perfect end to a winter's day.

EQUIPMENT

+ **Heavy-bottomed saucepan**
+ **Highball glass**

INGREDIENTS

+ **60 ml (2 fl oz) Fireball whisky**
+ **60 ml (2 fl oz) vanilla vodka**
+ **120 ml (4 fl oz) cloudy apple juice**
+ **Sliced, dried apple, to serve**

METHOD

Combine the whisky and vodka directly in the glass.

Gently heat the apple juice in a heavy-bottomed saucepan until warmed through and pour over the alcohol.

Garnish with sliced apple.

Lassi

The Lassi is a non-alcoholic yoghurt drink from the Indian subcontinent. This drink has endless possible variations, giving Sagittarius risings the range they crave.

EQUIPMENT

- ✦ Blender
- ✦ Old-fashioned glass, chilled

INGREDIENTS

- ✦ 120 ml (4 fl oz) plain yoghurt
- ✦ 3 ice cubes
- ✦ 80 ml (2⅓ fl oz) whole milk
- ✦ 25 g (1 oz) soft brown sugar, plus more to garnish
- ✦ 15 ml (½ fl oz) double cream
- ✦ 3 pistachio nuts, crushed, to garnish

METHOD

Blitz ingredients together until combined.

The speedy blending will mean the drink naturally froths at the top once poured out.

Sprinkle pinch of brown sugar and nuts over top of drink and serve.

Neapolitan Shooter

This ice-cream-themed shooter is perfect for Sagittarius moons who can't pick just one flavour. Garnish with a small chocolate-sandwich cookie (another great source of energy).

EQUIPMENT
+ **Long shot glass**

INGREDIENTS
+ **30 ml (1 fl oz) tequila rose**
+ **30 ml (1 fl oz) crème de cacao**
+ **30 ml (1 fl oz) Irish cream liqueur**
+ **Chocolate-sandwich cookie to serve**

METHOD

Carefully pour first the tequila rose, then the crème de cacao, then the Irish cream liqueur into a long shot glass, preserving the layers.

Serve with the sandwich cookie.

These shooters look very striking laid out in rows for a party.

Capricorn
(22 DECEMBER – 19 JANUARY)

RULING PLANET: SATURN
ELEMENT: EARTH

✦✦ Sun Sign: Overview ✦✦

The road may be steep and rocky but a sun-sign Capricorn will always find a way to succeed. First you'll create a meticulous plan, then you'll execute it to the last detail. And, it works! You are confident in your own skills, although this confidence can lead you to discard input from others. All we're saying is that you feel the need to be the one who chooses the cocktail bar! Another thing that surprises new acquaintances is that, although you're not loud and never boastful, you are ambitious.

PERSONALITY

You have all the right traits to help you achieve the success that you desire. You are trustworthy, disciplined and you don't give up easily. You see the world through a practical lens, every scenario something to be broken down into its parts and worked through sequentially. Your faith in this approach can make you headstrong and pretty stubborn once you've made a decision. Although you may not enjoy asking for help, you know when it's called for. You dislike breaking someone's trust and take pains to avoid it.

LOVE AND RELATIONSHIPS

You take pleasure in completing a process and following the rules. This makes you the champion of the courtship period. The wining, the dining, the little gifts, the charming moments – when it comes to dating you don't miss a trick. It's best for you to avoid reading too many listicles about dating practice because you can get sucked into trying to follow *all* the rules – even the contradictory ones. Remember that, just like life, love is what you make of it. You can make your own rules.

Your friendship flourishes with people who can be flexible and know how to compromise. Your hard head leads you to quickly reach an impasse with other stubborn star signs, such as Cancerians. You've never left a friend in the lurch. If there's an awkward moment at a party, you'll save them. If there's a box to be moved, you'll lift it. However, you're more than a reliable pair of hands. Your attention to detail means you always remember your friends' preferences and you have a great memory for shared moments.

✦ Rising Sign: Overview ✦

Capricorn rising signs are prone to caution. But, you often find that caution pays! You might not be the first person to pick up a new trend or to speak up when problem solving, but you're using that time wisely. You'll analyze the situation and make the move you want to make when the time is right. These tactics work for you, and when you deploy them you have a high success rate. So, why not be a little braver when relaying your talents?

✦ Moon Sign: Overview ✦

As an earth sign, Capricorn moons value the real and tangible. You like actions and results that you can see, feel and measure. This can be the hug between friends, a gift from a lover or the treat that you buy yourself after a successful project is completed. You have a strong connection with nature – simple gestures such as walking barefoot on grass can keep you grounded and soothe inner turmoil. You're not prone to easy emotional expression and some loved ones have to work harder than they'd like to pry out your feelings.

Incognito

The humble Capricorn sun sign enjoys passing under the radar. You could say they enjoy going... incognito.

EQUIPMENT

+ **Cocktail shaker, filled with ice**
+ **Strainer**
+ **Martini glass, chilled**

INGREDIENTS

+ **60 ml (2 fl oz) dry vermouth**
+ **60 ml (2 fl oz) cognac**
+ **45 ml (1½ fl oz) apricot brandy**
+ **3 dashes Angostura bitters**

METHOD

Combine the ingredients in the cocktail shaker.

Shake well and strain into a Martini glass.

This cocktail is so powerful you can be sure you won't miss the effects.

Virgin Piña Colada

Stubborn Capricorn suns might find it hard to believe that a Virgin Piña Colada can be as good as the original, but this recipe will convert you.

EQUIPMENT
- ✦ **Blender**
- ✦ **Hurricane glass, chilled**

INGREDIENTS
- ✦ **120 ml (4 fl oz) coconut cream**
- ✦ **15 ml (½ fl oz) double cream**
- ✦ **200 ml (6⅔ fl oz) pineapple juice**
- ✦ **Slice of pineapple**
- ✦ **Handful of ice**
- ✦ **Maraschino cherry, to garnish**

METHOD

Blitz all the ingredients except the cherry in a blender on the highest speed for 1 minute.

Pour into hurricane glass and garnish with maraschino cherry.

Enjoy the sunshine, or attempt to get caught in the rain.

Snowball

When you shake this cocktail up, it transforms into something frothy and exciting. Serve this to your date whenever you feel the need to change up your courting routine.

EQUIPMENT

+ **Cocktail shaker, filled with ice**
+ **Strainer**
+ **Highball glass**

INGREDIENTS

+ **60 ml (2 fl oz) advocaat**
+ **30 ml (1 fl oz) lime cordial**
+ **Lemonade to top**
+ **Maraschino cherry, on a cocktail stick, to serve**

METHOD

Add the ingredients to a cocktail shaker and shake briskly, but not overlong, until you create a frothy top.

Pour into the glass.

Balance the cherry and cocktail stick on the rim of the glass.

Cosmopolitan

The iconic pink of the Cosmopolitan was inspired by the colour of the sunrise of its birthplace, South Beach, Miami. It's the perfect cocktail for a Capricorn rising: a tangible – and tasty – representation of ephemeral beauty.

EQUIPMENT
+ **Cocktail shaker, filled with ice**
+ **Strainer**
+ **Martini glass, chilled**

INGREDIENTS
+ **30 ml (1 fl oz) vodka**
+ **30 ml (1 fl oz) triple sec**
+ **180 ml (6 fl oz) cranberry juice**
+ **30 ml (1 fl oz) lime juice, freshly squeezed**

METHOD

Combine the ingredients in a cocktail shaker and shake well.

Strain into Martini glass.

Like most short cocktails, Cosmopolitans are best consumed while still ice cold.

English Garden

This long drink is designed to bring all of the fresh beauty of a summer garden inside and into your glass. The perfect nectar for nature-loving Capricorn moons.

EQUIPMENT

- ✦ **Cocktail shaker, filled with ice**
- ✦ **Strainer**
- ✦ **Highball glass, filled with ice**

INGREDIENTS

- ✦ **60 ml (2 fl oz) gin**
- ✦ **150 ml (5 fl oz) cloudy apple juice**
- ✦ **30 ml (1 fl oz) elderflower cordial**
- ✦ **30 ml (1 fl oz) lime juice, freshly squeezed**
- ✦ **Handful mint leaves to garnish**

METHOD

Add the liquid ingredients to the cocktail shaker.

Shake until combined, then strain into glass.

Garnish with mint leaves.

Aquarius

(20 JANUARY – 18 FEBRUARY)

RULING PLANET: URANUS
ELEMENT: AIR

✦ Sun Sign: Overview ✦

Aquarian sun signs are not afraid to stand out from the crowd. Others may have a box they want to put you in, labelled eccentric or quirky, but you know that you defy such definitions – you're just yourself. You have a ravenous curiosity and are always searching for your newest favourite cocktail. You're so excited by what you can learn from others that you sometimes forget to share something of yourself in return. This can lead to friends and loved ones feeling their connection with you isn't as strong as they'd like it to be.

PERSONALITY

You channel your eclectic knowledge into a powerful creative force. You enjoy applying it to problems of now and the future. You visualize the big picture and you know that someone need only apply a little innovation and forward-thinking to make it happen. Your belief in the possibility of positive change is beguiling, so much so that you can become disappointed and bitter if things don't work out as you had hoped. You don't mesh well with authority and you certainly don't like others attempting to impose their will on you.

LOVE AND RELATIONSHIPS

You need a partner that gives you room to grow. You're interested in a love that is centred around adventure and progress. Lovers who require obvious shows of affection may feel insecure around your subtle love languages. However, you really are generous with the respect you show and trust you give your loved ones. You prefer romance to spring up organically, perhaps from an existing friendship – the formal dating scene makes you uncomfortable.

You take a humanitarian view of the world and the people in it. There are very few people that you wouldn't greet with a smile and an open mind. Acquaintances quickly turn into friends. One of the only times that you feel reserve toward someone is if you witness the kind of snobbery or suspicion that you yourself are so unfamiliar with. You love to debate and parry and get everything you can out of the relationship. However, you treat everything with such lightness that you sometimes breeze on to your next conversation and aren't aware that you've left behind questions or hurt feelings.

⭐ Rising Sign: Overview ⭐

Aquarius rising signs don't just foresee change; they help create change. You aren't interested in conforming to society, which gives you an ability to see what changes are needed. You're always ready to delve deep into any topic with anyone who is around you. Many are inspired by your innovative ideas but some bristle at your perspective. You value your own difference and that gives you a self-assured confidence in the face of conformist critique. However, you can fall into the trap of looking so hard for the difference between you and the people around you that you forget to find the common ground you share.

⭐ Moon Sign: Overview ⭐

You desire connection with others and almost everything about you paves the way for it. You're open, incredibly accepting and able to see the best in anyone. So, what's holding you back? Truth be told, your reluctance to open up emotionally is stunting the growth of deeper bonds with those you admire. You're drawn to the outsider roles in society and have a deep distrust of systems and authority.

Leave It to Me No. 1

"Leave it to me" is practically the Aquarius sun's motto. You love mulling over a problem and visualizing how you can fix it. Apply yourself to this cocktail and see how it goes.

EQUIPMENT

+ **Cocktail shaker, filled with ice**
+ **Strainer**
+ **Martini glass, chilled**

INGREDIENTS

+ **60 ml (2 fl oz) gin**
+ **30 ml (1 fl oz) apricot brandy**
+ **30 ml (1 fl oz) dry vermouth**
+ **Dash lemon juice, freshly squeezed**
+ **Dash grenadine**

METHOD

Shake the ingredients in the cocktail shaker.

Strain into Martini glass.

This is a good alternative to a sour for those who don't like raw egg.

Rainbow Paradise

This rainbow recipe is a bold choice, perfect for Aquarius suns who thrive on standing out from the crowd.

EQUIPMENT

+ **Hurricane glass, filled with ice**
+ **Bar spoon**

INGREDIENTS

+ **60 ml (2 fl oz) grenadine, plus a dash**
+ **240 ml (8 fl oz) pineapple juice**
+ **60 ml (2 fl oz) white rum**
+ **40 ml (1⅓ fl oz) blue curaçao**

METHOD

Pour the grenadine into the glass.

Mix the pineapple juice and white rum separately and split into two.

Add a dash of grenadine to the first batch of pineapple and rum and stir to create an orange hue. Gently layer on top of grenadine in hurricane glass.

Gently layer second batch of pineapple and rum in hurricane glass.

Layer blue curaçao on top.

Blue Lagoon Mocktail

The deep blue of this mocktail is like the water of life. Use this to nourish the small tendrils of organic-relationship growth that you crave.

EQUIPMENT

+ **Highball glass, half-filled with ice**
+ **Bar spoon**

INGREDIENTS

+ **125 ml (4⅓ fl oz) blue curaçao syrup**
+ **30 ml (1 fl oz) lemon juice, freshly squeezed**
+ **Lemon-lime soda, to top**
+ **Lemon slice, to garnish**

METHOD

Pour the syrup and lemon juice into the glass and stir vigorously to combine.

Gently pour over the lemon-lime soda and carefully stir several times until combined.

Pop the slice of lemon on top, like the sunshine over a lake.

E.T.

—

This layered shooter is pretty out there. In fact, it's like nothing on this earth – just like an Aquarius rising sign. And of course, E.T. stands for Extra Tasty...

EQUIPMENT
+ **Long shot glass, chilled**

INGREDIENTS
+ **30 ml (1 fl oz) vodka**
+ **30 ml (1 fl oz) Irish cream liqueur**
+ **30 ml (1 fl oz) melon liqueur**

METHOD

Carefully layer the ingredients in the shot glass.

Pour the vodka first, then the Irish cream, then the melon liqueur.

Start your engines, because this shooter will have you off like a rocket.

Crocodile

The Crocodile is a cocktail beloved of anarchists in the late-nineteenth century, according to Thomas Pynchon's novel *Against the Day*. Although not every Aquarius moon is a social revolutionary, you are one of the few who has the same strong stomach for this wild cocktail.

EQUIPMENT

+ **Bar spoon**
+ **Old-fashioned glass, filled with ice**

INGREDIENTS

+ **30 ml (1 fl oz) absinthe**
+ **30 ml (1 fl oz) brandy**
+ **30 ml (1 fl oz) rum**
+ **60 ml (2 fl oz) cream**

METHOD

Gently pour the ingredients over the ice and stir.

If you can survive this recipe, you're ready for the revolution.

Pisces

(19 FEBRUARY – 20 MARCH)

RULING PLANET: NEPTUNE
ELEMENT: WATER

⋆ Sun Sign: Overview ⋆

The intuitive, creative Pisces sun sign drifts through a pleasant world of their own making. You are compassionate and see the best in the people and the world around you. You don't hold on to grudges or linger on unpleasant memories; you simply keep swimming towards the lighter, brighter future. Your preference for all things pleasant does make you wary of the tough but right thing to do, meaning you sometimes lose out in the long term. You express yourself through creativity and enjoy making cocktails.

PERSONALITY

You are gentle, living half your time in a dream world. Your capacity for understanding others' perspectives is enormous and that leads to strong relationships with diverse groups of people. However, your tendency to go for gut-feeling over analysis can lead you to be over-trusting, and sometimes taken advantage of. Living in dreamland can lead you to have unrealistic expectations of the world around you, but it is just as likely to help you envision ways to bring more beauty and positivity to your life.

LOVE AND RELATIONSHIPS

Pisces sun sign is a modern-day poet, brimming with emotion. You are romantic and offer love with all the trappings. You put yourself at the disposal of the ones you love, ready to support them however they need it most. With so much to give, why don't you get snapped up immediately by potential partners? You can be a little shy and therefore slow to open up. Once you've opened up, you have no qualms about sharing what's on your mind and in your heart.

You need a friend that can help you turn your dreams into reality. You enjoy spending time with fellow imaginers but you can't deny that you need someone with a little oomph to get things going. You're drawn to friends who possess analytical minds and practical powers – you enjoy seeing how they transform what might be into what is. You don't mesh so well with people with endless get up and go. Many Pisceans are introverts, so although you enjoy the company of friends, it helps to schedule a little "recharge" time after a run of social activity.

✶✶ Rising Sign: Overview ✶✶

Pisces rising signs' roving dreams can have an impact on their emotional outlook. They are like a swiftly changing sky: clouds cover the sun and darken their mood and, just as quickly, they are gone. You largely internalize these shifts in mood. You'll only express your negative emotions in the most extreme circumstances because you much prefer to stay quiet and pass largely unnoticed. You live gently and desire to bring joy to anywhere you can have an impact. You are observant and like to reflect on what you see before passing judgement.

✶✶ Moon Sign: Overview ✶✶

Moon-sign Pisceans vibrate on whichever wavelength they come into contact with. This gives you a tremendous capacity for empathy; you can completely comprehend other people's perspective and emotions. So much so that your own identity is sometimes eclipsed. What seemed like strongly held personal opinions can be swayed or transformed first by one person, then another. What doesn't change is your passion for creative expression. You show the world your internal feelings through the arts, such as music, painting or writing.

Golden Dream

Pisces sun's dreams come in many shades, but this one is golden. It's a transformation of the tough-spirited Martini into something creamy and vanilla-infused.

EQUIPMENT

- ✦ **Cocktail shaker, filled with ice**
- ✦ **Strainer**
- ✦ **Martini glass, chilled**

INGREDIENTS

- ✦ **40 ml (1⅓ fl oz) triple sec**
- ✦ **40 ml (1⅓ fl oz) vanilla vodka liqueur**
- ✦ **40 ml (1⅓ fl oz) cream**
- ✦ **40 ml (1⅓ fl oz) orange juice**

METHOD

Put the ingredients in the cocktail shaker and shake to combine, using a little extra strength to avoid the citrus acid of the orange juice splitting the cream.

Strain into the Martini glass.

Enjoy this adult version of an orange ice-cream lolly.

Açaí Smoothie

The açaí fruit is a tropical berry that lends a rich, purple hue to its delicious recipes. This non-alcoholic, healthy smoothie will help your body become in tune with nature.

EQUIPMENT
+ **Blender**
+ **Highball glass, chilled**

INGREDIENTS
+ **20 g (⅓ oz) açaí powder**
+ **250 g (8⅔ oz) frozen mixed berries**
+ **1 frozen banana**
+ **130 ml (4⅓ fl oz) oat milk**
+ **2 ice cubes**

METHOD

Combine the ingredients in a blender and blitz on a high speed until fully combined.

Add a splash more milk if the mixture looks like it is too thick to be drinkable.

Pour into a glass.

The Last Word

This prohibition-era gin cocktail was once lost and has risen to popularity since being rediscovered. Shy Pisces suns could do with trying to get the last word in a bit more often - see if this recipe will inspire you.

EQUIPMENT

+ Cocktail shaker, filled with ice
+ Strainer
+ Coupe glass, chilled

INGREDIENTS

+ 30 ml (1 fl oz) gin
+ 30 ml (1 fl oz) chartreuse
+ 30 ml (1 fl oz) maraschino liqueur
+ 30 ml (1 fl oz) lime juice
+ Maraschino cherry, to garnish

METHOD

Shake the ingredients, except the cherry, together in a cocktail shaker.

Strain into a coupe glass.

Garnish with jaunty maraschino cherry.

Dark and Stormy Punch

Dark and Stormy cocktails are a classic combination of rum and ginger beer that matches the shifting moods of a Pisces rising. Fiery at first, you'll be sweet by the next sip.

EQUIPMENT

+ **Jug, filled with ice**
+ **Muddler**

INGREDIENTS

+ **300 g (10½ oz) pineapple, cut into chunks**
+ **300 ml (10 fl oz) spiced rum**
+ **Juice of 1 lime**
+ **Pinch of grated nutmeg**
+ **Pinch of ground cinnamon**
+ **Pinch of ground ginger**
+ **Fiery ginger beer, to top**
+ **Lime, cut into wedges, to serve**

METHOD

Muddle the pineapple, rum, lime juice and spices until the pineapple is partially crushed and has released its juices.

Add the lime wedges and gently top with ginger beer.

Death in the Afternoon

As avid artists, Pisces moon signs should drink like an artist. Hemingway was one of the world's greatest writers and most prolific drinkers. He invented this cocktail and named it after one of his most famous works.

EQUIPMENT
+ **Cocktail shaker, filled with ice**
+ **Strainer**
+ **Coupe glass, chilled**

INGREDIENTS
+ **30 ml (1 fl oz) absinthe**
+ **Champagne to top**

METHOD

Shake the absinthe in the cocktail shaker and strain into the coupe glass.

Gently top up with champagne.

Hemingway enjoyed his drinks ice-cold, so consume straight away.

⋆✦ Farewell ✦⋆

Now you've learned a little more about yourself and, hopefully, a lot more about cocktails! You can use the recipes in this book for more than just treating yourself. You could design a night with your closest friends, offering them each a bespoke cocktail. Or you could theme your birthday celebrations around a cocktail that stands out to you.

Just like the celestial bodies that dance across the sky, you are always changing. If a once-favourite cocktail stops resonating with you, dip back into this little guide to find the recipe that best suits your evolved self.

Remember, your next cocktail may be written in the stars!

# Resources

WEBSITES

astro.com
newparadigmastrology.com
linda-goodman.com
astrologyzone.com

BOOKS

Birkbeck, Lyn *The Instant Astrologer* (2003, O Books)

Goodman, Linda *Sun Signs* (1999, Pan)

Greene, Liz *Astrology for Lovers* (1999, Thorsons)

Mann, A. T. *The Round Art* (2003, Vega Books)

Parker, Derek and Julia *Astrology* (1994, Dorling Kindersley)

Pelletier, Robert *Planets in Aspect* (1987, Schiffer)

Williamson, Marion *The Little Book of the Zodiac* (2018, Summersdale)

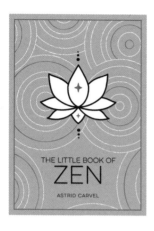

The Little Book of Zen

Astrid Carvel

ISBN: 978-1-80007-197-1

Zen is a philosophy for living in a state of kindness, gratitude and awareness, teaching us to be present and to experience the world as it truly is. This book will reveal how you can apply the principles of Zen to your daily life and reap the benefits to gain a greater sense of peace and calm. Through simple tips, guided meditations and thought exercises, you can learn to cultivate Zen, whether you're new to the practice or have been familiar with it for years.

The Little Book of Goddesses

Astrid Carvel

ISBN: 978-1-80007-198-8

Embrace the power of the divine in this beginner's guide to some of mythology's fiercest females and most legendary ladies. Learn about Athena, the Greek goddess of wisdom and war; Bastet, the Egyptian goddess of pleasure and protection; Freyja, the Norse goddess of love, and many others. You'll be inspired and empowered by the tales of feminine power, strength and wisdom of all these dazzling deities.

Have you enjoyed this book?
If so, find us on Facebook at
Summersdale Publishers, on Twitter
at **@Summersdale** and on Instagram
at **@summersdalebooks** and get in touch.
We'd love to hear from you!

www.summersdale.com

Image credits

Chapter title page illustration © Tanya Antusenok/Shutterstock.com
Zodiac symbols throughout © maryannacher/Shutterstock.com
Cocktail illustrations throughout © SurfsUp/Shutterstock.com
Hand drawn cocktails throughout © Net Vector/Shutterstock.com
Drinks illustrations throughout © mamita/Shutterstock.com
pp.67, 75, 112, 120 – highball cocktail © alya_haciyeva/Shutterstock.com